THIS SIDE OF UTOPIA

Thad DeVassie

Červená Barva Press
Somerville, Massachusetts

Červená Barva Press
P.O. Box 440357
W. Somerville, MA 02144-3222

www.cervenabarvapress.com
Bookstore: www.thelostbookshelf.com

Cover art: "Before the Fall" by Thad DeVassie

Cover Design: William J. Kelle
Production: Steve Asmussen

ISBN: 978-1-950063-67-3

Contents

THIS SIDE OF UTOPIA

For my mother, Lola Faye

I'll see you on the other side.

When I wrote my early poems "Knife," "Fork," and "Spoon," in 1964, I lived on 13th St. and University Place [in Manhattan] in a little dump of an apartment. It was summer, and I'd eaten something. I was looking at the table at the knife, the fork, and the spoon. And I noticed how interesting these three were. I'd stolen one from a greasy spoon, and another from somewhere else. I remember thinking, "Well, Mr. Simic, let's see if you can write a poem about this." Because no one had ever written a poem about a fork, or a knife, although we have to use them every day.

So I wrote them, and I sent them to a magazine called *The Quarterly Review of Literature*. The editor wrote to me and rejected the poems saying "Dear Mr. Simic ... you obviously sound like an intelligent young man."

Which sort of puzzled me—I thought, "What the f*** does he know?" He said, "Why do you write poems about these things? Why do you write about such inconsequential things as silverware utensils?"

I came into the library with that letter, feeling both annoyed—I mean, thinking *you idiot! Should I write about sunsets in June?*—and at the same time I felt triumphant. I thought, *well, this is what I'm going to do from now on. This is my thing.* I felt I was on the right track.

—Charles Simic

Interviewed by Joe Fassler for The Atlantic

May 6, 2015

Table Manners

"…and the dish ran away with the spoon."
—Mother Goose nursery rhyme

After serving up the Littles – both Jack Horner
and Miss Muffet – Mother takes us around

the mulberry bush squawking endless tales
of domestic and barnyard hijinks.

But spilling the flatware affair…
what could've prompted such gossip

that in time all children learn to recite?
Was it out of spite for a Canadian lover

who flew south for greener pastures?
Give it time. Fork and saucer will piece it

together, see each other across
a less-crowded table, Yin missing

its Yang, and then conspire
with knife to set things right.

Homesick

As I walked the streets of Siena I found myself
craving Chinese takeout from the old neighborhood,
chopsticks in a paper sleeve, sticky rice in a box.

On the lawn in Pisa where I ate a quick bite of lunch,
I fancied the tower razed, its dilapidated state
reminding me of my study, it too on the brink of ruin.

On a gondola in Venice, I felt my heart pang
for my city ripe with its own smells, for a taxi
ride void of any whiff or appearance of romance.

In Rome's piazzas, and especially at the Trevi Fountain,
I wished someone who was making a wish would wish
that my wish would come true. When you asked me

what I wished for, I couldn't bring myself to say I longed
to be at home eating Kung Pao chicken in my study, thumbing
through a tour brochure of Italy, dreaming of what it must be like.

Let's Call This Something
Other Than What It Is

A man (let's call him Carl) places a flash drive in a bottle, corks it
and then chucks it into the ocean (let's call this romantic, or foolish).

Carl forgets about this lark of an experiment as the bottle continues
its slow journey to a distant shoreline (let's call this the opposite of
instant gratification).

A woman (let's call her Carla) finds Carl's bottle (let's call this suspen-
sion of reality), and removes the flash drive with no note (let's call this
peculiar given the amount of storage).

Carla is incapable of opening the contents of the drive (let's call this,
for a lack of a better word, suspense) but has shared the news of her
finding

with her friend (let's call him Kopaz) who happens to work at the local
police station (let's call this foreshadowing). Kopaz has connections
(let's call this obvious)

and manages to open all the files on Carl's drive in hopes of under-
standing the purpose of its extraordinary journey. It appears Carl is in
search of love

by leveraging today's technology (let's call this acceptable or, for sake
of argument, a sign of the times). Carla is mildly intrigued. Carl has
posted many pictures of himself

from a social media platform. OMG. TMI. (let's call this reality teeter-
ing on creepy). Carla is less intrigued. It becomes clear that Carl does
not understand boundaries or

common decency with the use of these technologies (let's call this
disturbing). Kopaz is now intrigued (let's call this his 15 minutes of
fame). Carl gets a knock

on the door (let's call this inevitable). Carl is in trouble (let's call this his 15 minutes of fame or, again, foolish). Carl finds himself in a mini-mum-security facility

(let's call this fate). With great remorse, Carl sends a handwritten letter to Carla for his foolishness and this whole misunderstanding (let's call this irony).

Improvement District

There are no more storefront windows.
No place for peering, for wishful thinking.
Cockroaches and punch clocks, the slab
out back for a smoke – they all remain.

But gone are the storefront windows,

and there are children who are none
the wiser. They have grown with aisles
of toys stacked ceiling high in warehouse
fashion, Barbie beside her dream house,

it too, abounding with faux windows.

Downtown is boarded up except for
pockets deemed revitalized. There,
well-pressed doormen slouch behind
granite and cherry workstations

viewing monitors, quick to tell every kid

to *move along, nothin' to see in here.*
But they're not after the *why* or the *how*
come, in search of a history lost. All they
care to know is what the doormen

watch on their tiny televisions.

The Naked Truth

Stand in the shower long enough
without a catchy song to sing
and the worst will come to mind.

Plug your ears and all you'll hear
is water pounding on the tin-like
roof of your balding head.

Pity the washcloth
as it takes a cruise around
your unmentionables.

You cannot shave the otter
from your face, you cannot scrub
the walrus from your frame.

This is the naked truth,
the problem with heavy thought
during the morning wash,

the reason for a strong melody
and out-of-tune vocals.
Make no mistake,

they are as necessary as soap,
as vital as the oversized towel
on the back of the door.

Amateur Cosmology

You are my mute and orange companion,
hovering along the convex wall of your tiny
round bowl atop this disheveled Pembroke table,

         reading my paper,

          transfixed to my telly

        with loyal monotony.

I question if you question when the laugh
track is off, when a show has jumped the shark,
if Ronco products are as good as advertised.

What if you're the Stephen Hawking of guppies,
a savant of a fish with accumulated knowledge
whose tiny o-like bubbles rising to the surface
can be decoded to reveal this brief history in time
for the good of the species?

It's a lot to philosophize before the net arrives,
before the commode lid is raised, before a final lap
in a windowless bowl reveals the Big Flush
and a black hole into oblivion.

Infinity's Loop

Infinity
the toppled
hourglass of eternity is
nothing more than a hopeless
romantic, just like us mortals, longing
for one true thing. Call it a search
for wisdom, an act of
stubbornness

even a glutton
for punishment – her ankles
swollen and blue from the endless
figure eights. Pity the plight but praise
her persistence, looping around
in that tireless, endless
pursuit of a happy
ending.

Do No Harm

I.
There is the early bird, then the lowly
worm. First, even at this hour we are told,
do no harm. For the unfortunate worm
there is no mulligan, just soaking rain,
then beaks. In the safety of dew-damp
trees, early birds feast on the meaning of harm.

II.
"There is safety in numbers"
implies that you, in the singular,
are prone to danger, as in leisurely
walks down dark alleys. Alone.
Nobody has ever been saved by pi,
rescued by a pack of integers.
Numbers that cling closely—
cholesterol, weight, my social—
all of which could heed the warning
from *first, do no harm.*

III.
"Objects in the mirror are closer
than they appear" was coined by engineers
then embraced by lawyers, one group
understanding *first, do no harm,*
recognizing the safety in numbers;
the other group adding the retort
"to [insert company name here]"
which led to "warning" "caution" and "!"
in attempt to save us first from ourselves,
the safety of someone else's numbers.

IV.
He's direct with me, even more so
in her absence. Hysterectomy. Proof
that we'll be lacking in numbers,
requisite safety. This fact will soon
sink in, hit close to home, closer
than it currently appears. I contemplate
medicine, its preventative qualities,
triumphs, what ifs, and how *do no harm*
applies to the woman about to enter
the room. I stumble on clichés,
wondering if misery loves company,
if a good man is hard to find.

V.
Each day we die a little,
then a little more. This is harm's
true equation, the continuous flow
of sand through time's bottleneck.
Each blessing we count is a fraction
of the little that is lost, for which
there is seldom any blessing.

VI.
Hippocrates did not claim
it first nor was it his oath.
He hedged his bets on the idea
to help, or *at least* do no harm,
which is far from first.
It is one way of worming out
of moral absolutism, at the least.
He preferred "early riser"

to the perfunctory early bird
for reasons ripe with speculation.

VII.
Hype is to hyper as hysteria applies
to the woman who has entered the room.
This was Hippocrates' first, even if
misguided. I will be the good man,
committed to the *at least,* to do no harm.
What happens first or next is anyone's guess.

Barber School Haircut

I remember Cal from the city morgue telling me how cadavers were useful learning tools, familiarizing young med students with the ins and outs of the human body without the pressure of a patient in distress.

I think of my old pal, himself a well-groomed gent, recalling his comments as I watch instructors scurry the floor with scissors in hand, clippers in turquoise blue smocks, bailing out barbers-to-be, treating customers like distraught patients as they learn of their new horror with a swivel of the chair.

When I die, my hair will be the envy of many, my embalmer patient and unconcerned with flipping his chair. But here and now we still sit, this assemblage of haggard men and unkempt children, cross-legged and concerned on a row of teal enamel chairs, quietly contemplating what we know could be a grave mistake.

Evel Knievel's Comeback World Tour Hits a Snag

Somewhere on the Dark Continent he traveled a dirt road into a tiny village resembling a patchwork American flag on two wheels. A pack of boys pointed and yelled "the evil one!" at which he downshifted and waved at the false jubilation of his name.

The pack of boys, who quickly circled like blood-thirsty dogs, moved in for the kill and pulled the chrome tailpipe from his nimble Honda, beat his ride to a pulp as they chanted "*little Mogadishu!*" around his cowering body, atop his mangled bike.

He waved his sequined cape as if to call a truce. He offered to arm wrestle them for his possessions. He even claimed to be George Hamilton, his dramatic made-for-TV counterpart – anything to avoid another broken pelvis.

His ill-fated comeback was unfolding in a world he no longer knew.

Meanwhile, on the outskirts of that tiny village, a small but spirited group of villagers remain stumped on how to get four dozen goats lined up between two bamboo ramps.

Doll Factory

It is somewhere
the cartographers paid
little attention to

or flatly overlooked:
a small nameless dot
familiar to capitalists

and desperate migrants.
Inside, bins of smiling
porous doll heads await,

as if to say, adorn us,
as synthetic hair begins
to grow. Stacks of arms

wave at torsos tumbling
down the line. News flows
slow and dreams row

at conveyor belt pace,
in contrast to the hysteria
in suburbia's toy store aisles,

where girls melt down,
confident as capitalists,
believing this doll

is *the* answer,
the one to put her dreams
on the map.

Matryoshka Dolls

With broken English and calloused hands
she speaks of history and dank poverty,

of delusion and dreams misguided.
Her peasant existence is in stark contrast

to the rich patina of her handiwork.
Her nesting dolls feature notable tyrants

of corruption and oppression cloaked
within the tall facsimile and smirk of Stalin,

his thick mustache resembling a compact
black coffin above his flat-lined lips.

Beneath his figure lies more regimes,
each idealist pried open to find another:

Chairman Mao, Hitler, Mussolini.
Deeper still is Hussein, Ho Chi Minh.

Cracking Milosevic exposes a small Pol Pot,
a tiny Pinochet who harbors the first couple

of Authoritarianism, Ferdinand and Imelda,
with Ms. Marcos being at the core, ever so

small and hapless like a poor peasant girl
for whom there are no shoes.

Modern Conveniences

Giraffe gently transferred the pipe wrench from her mouth
to my outstretched hand. The baboons snickered

with the lemurs over the meticulousness of such
pointless plumbing. Hyena said nothing, in part because

a desolate desert is no laughing matter. The commode,
with its series of snaking pipes, copper fittings

and galvanized nipples, looked like a deepwater
octopus turned amphibian, proudly sitting

in the sand with its seat up, privately yearning
for a wash basin, its porcelain companion.

Then prairie dog, propped on his hind legs, stated the obvious
to the chagrin of camel: *"There's no water within 20 miles of here."*

I could see the perspiration beading on camel's hump, fear
of shoddy logistics and bush-league navigation about to be

exposed on his watch. But then ostrich buried her head deep
into the bowl and everyone agreed we were on to something.

A Sharp Saw

Several people in parkas sat impatiently on folding chairs.
A man in the front row wore a babushka hat, but no
breath was visible. Everyone held it, anticipating

the miraculous to occur. I stood on a small makeshift stage
holding a sharp saw. A female stagehand of average size
and modest looks kept nodding as if we shared

a mutual unspoken language. She moved toward me and climbed
into a pine box to murmurs of *Oh Dear God!* as a commotion
of chairs quickly followed. Her unspoken language pelted me

with profanities as she shut the lid, her head in the clear
and feet pushed through tiny round holes. Troubling thoughts
swirled my head: *Who is this woman? I'm no magician.*

With or against the grain? As the man in the babushka hat got up
to leave, I felt her tug my trousers and offer up a curt whisper,
below the line, take it below the bikini line.

Domestic Affairs

You are the pot roast. I am the rake.

These are not a social scientist's labels for purposes of categorization, nor do they represent gender-based biases of bygone eras. You, indeed, are a pot roast. I am a rake.

Lyndon B. Johnson's ghost is eavesdropping on how we navigate our foreign policy.

Our lawn has been replaced with floor tiles from a Vatican outbuilding. We can neither count nor estimate the number of feet that have trampled over them in either state. To suggest this emasculates me, does.

Our lawnmower is enshrined in a shed titled *things we once used.* You hammered a solitary nail into a beam from which nothing yet hangs. This is your preparatory nature.

Our children are crickets, small and symbolically quiet, unable to compose the beautiful noise they are meant to make. If only we knew how to teach them our strange musicology.

I remind you, as lovingly as a rake can, that when I say *'you haven't the grit it takes'* I'm not being metaphorical. Or facetious. We simply have different etymologies.

We could make light of your tenderness, my harshness as others did. As others do. As others.

You say you are dying in perpetuity and not to let what lingers between us deceive; to know what is real. I carry death in my teeth, always. This is my destiny. No wonder we're soulmates.

Billy Doesn't Live Here

It's early and, admittedly, I hate early,
so I fight the urge to retreat back
to bed, boil some water for tea

and, calm as a lake in its carafe, I pour
what's left of last night's coffee and wait.
Clearly, this is not a Billy Collins poem,

but it doesn't stop me from trying to find
a window, one with a view of rolling fields
or capable birds that surely enjoy early,

yet all I have is a panorama of this
darkened alley, a flickering streetlight
and a posse of masked raccoons sifting

through my neighbor's garbage. Make no
mistake, Mr. Collins lives neither in this
poem nor on the other side of the alley.

The water is slow to boil but the burner
has scorched drippings of some long-forgotten
sauce, my smoke alarm now mimicking

the screech-chirp of some ancient, ill-fated
pterodactyl while I ponder if those raccoons
have just found a sack of rotten apples or

mealy potatoes, neither of which I can recall
making a cameo in a Collins poem. I want
to pick up an old rotary phone and dial

charming Billy, ask him how he does it
each morning with all that silence,
the dew and the frost, all that tea and coffee

without a single mention of the latrine,
and the poem that rolls right out of bed
like the actress who needs no primping.

We Live Here So You Could Visit

Museum placards are etched with names
of the never to be known. There isn't a single
sports franchise, a stadium, or rabid fan base.
Neatly manicured parks contain equipment

manufactured in defunct factories from elsewhere
and generations behind the times. Mountain ranges,
coastlines, and inland lakes are foreign to our neck
of woods, which also is lacking in meaningful abundance.

Downtown streets fold up long before dusk.
On Sundays, commerce flows from its weekday trickle
to a drought-like halt. Streetlamps magnify the wet sorrow
of a city left behind during summer rain.

The deadening silence of inactivity, a town fast asleep
without assurance of an alarm, amplifies one's ability to hear
their beating heart, feel blood coursing through veins,
signaling life while cutting against the grain of progress.

Maybe it's the charm of not being overly charming,
or being the forgotten cog that has fallen
from the advancing machine that summons
the smallest of affections, which is enough

to remind us why we stay here and hold dear
to what once was, in its non-homogeneous beauty,
coupled with the recurring promise of what may lie
ahead without disappointment of ever knowing the truth.

Field Trip to the Mall

From this distance Lincoln appears to be slouching
in his chair, as if defeated at what he must cast his eyes
upon with each new sunrise. Snaking monuments

of war that children, newly released from classrooms,
trudge alongside with paper and lead in hand, searching
for surnames perfectly etched. Some hold their tongues

as told while others see their faces captured in slabs
of black granite. Like miniature mothers, small bands
of brothers, they mutely reflect generations past.

They carry on quietly with interlocked hands toward
the National Gallery of Art, across a stretch of grass
reserved for a future shrine of conflict, many marching

in unison with a soldier's sure footing
while others are dragged away protesting,
looking over their small shoulders in despair.

The Great Unknown

It is hard at work
maintaining anonymity,
toiling near obscurity's
darkest border in a soot-dusted
miner's helmet and cloak
of vagueness, out of reach
of the lanterned, canteened,
and long-since skeletoned
where such detritus holds
magnetic lure, mythic lore.

If they knew
it was reduced
to un

      -spectacular
      -worthy
      -interesting
      -done

and akin to suburban Wichita,
who would embark on searches
for ordinary, let alone expeditions
toward the great ordinary?

Cricket Hymn for the Apocalypse

In the distance, we hear crickets
rolling up in their makeshift wheelchairs,
novices learning to play tiny violins.

Surely they don't know the murder ballads
or a single funeral march. How could they
with their repertoire amputated, all but erased?

Yet from this distance, it sounds as if
they are composing a gorgeous hymn
for the end of the world.

Acknowledgements

Grateful acknowledgement to the editors of the following publications where selected poems from this collection first appeared:

"Table Manners" — *PANK*
"Homesick" — *New York Quarterly*
"Let's Call This Something Other Than What It Is" — *FLASH: International Short Story Magazine*
"Improvement District" — *Poetry East*
"The Naked Truth" — *FLARE: The Flagler Review*
"Do No Harm" — *Santa Clara Review*
"Barber School Haircut" — *Concho River Review*
"Evel Knievel's Comeback World Tour Hits a Snag" — *Sentence: A Journal of Prose Poetics*
"Matryoshka Dolls" — *Junto Magazine*
"A Sharp Saw" — *Fox Cry Review*
"Billy Doesn't Live Here" — *Ampersand*
"We Live Here So You Could Visit" — *Pudding Magazine*
"Field Trip to the Mall" — *Collateral*
"Cricket Hymn for the Apocalypse" — *Fifty-Two Stories*

About the Author

Thad DeVassie is a poet and writer who pivots between traditional line breaks of poetry and a linear love of prose poetry, flash fiction, and creative nonfiction. In 2020 he was named a winner of the James Tate Poetry Prize for his manuscript *Splendid Irrationalities* (SurVision Books). In 2021, his project *Year Of Static*, containing 11 original paintings with accompanying micro prose, was published by Ghost City Press. It evolved into the art exhibition *Love Your Neighbor* in 2022. A lifelong Ohioan, Thad writes and paints from the outskirts of Columbus.

* 9 7 8 1 9 5 0 0 6 3 6 7 3 *